IMAGES
of England

SOUTH TELFORD
IRONBRIDGE GORGE,
MADELEY AND DAWLEY

Coalbrookdale born and bred. Betty Duddell outside Fountain Villa, Coalbrookdale in about 1924. Betty still lives in The Dale, only a 100 yards from Fountain Villa.

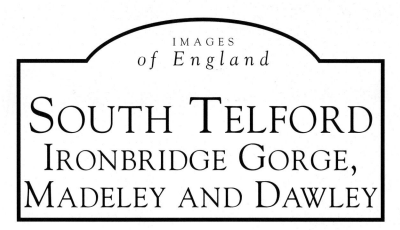

IMAGES
of England

SOUTH TELFORD
IRONBRIDGE GORGE,
MADELEY AND DAWLEY

Compiled by
John Powell and Michael A. Vanns

TEMPUS

The start of a new era and a new century in Dawley. The High Street decorated in celebration of King Edward VII's coronation in 1902.

First published 1995, reprinted 2003

Tempus Publishing Limited
The Mill, Brimscombe Port,
Stroud, Gloucestershire, GL5 2QG

British Library Cataloguing in Publication Data.
A catalogue record for this book is available from the British Library.

ISBN 0 7524 0125 4

Typesetting and origination by Tempus Publishing Limited
Printed in Great Britain by Midway Colour Print, Wiltshire

Contents

The stationmaster at Coalport Great Western Railway station in the 1920's is sporting military-style polished shoes. This was the station on the south side of the river, the main building now surviving as a private residence, although the line was closed in 1963.

Nineteenth century view of the Iron Bridge, looking downstream from the south bank of the river. The lantern was still in position on the centre of the bridge then, and the lack of trees compared to today is very noticeable.

Introduction

In the eighteenth and early nineteenth centuries, a series of technological breakthroughs occurred in and around Coalbrookdale which were to transform the ironmaking industry and earn for the locality the sobriquet "Birthplace of the Industrial Revolution". During the last three decades of the twentieth century, the names Ironbridge and Coalbrookdale have become known to hundreds of thousands of people from all over the world who have visited the monuments and museum sites which bear testimony to those remarkable achievements.

This volume, however, is not primarily concerned with either of these periods, but portrays South Telford during the 120 years or so which fall between the two. By the time the camera arrived on the scene, it was to record a district which, although still largely dependent on coal, iron and clay for its livelihood, could best be described as suffering a slow yet inevitable industrial decline. This process was to continue more or less unchecked until the coming of the New Town in the 1960's, bringing as it did new houses, new roads, new factories and new jobs.

The photographs contained in this book will appeal equally to the newcomer to South Telford, who wants to learn more about its past, and to the person born and bred locally who may wish to recall how it used to be. They are drawn almost entirely from the collection built up by the Library of the Ironbridge Gorge Museum Trust over the past 25 years, a collection which the compilers have been responsible for conserving, storing and indexing for much of that time. Many have been donated or lent for copying by local residents, to whom the Museum would like to express its heartfelt thanks. The choice of pictures has been a personal one, an attempt being made to strike a balance between those showing people and those showing places. Some will have been seen before, but many are published for the first time.

Coverage starts in Madeley, already an old-established town when Abraham Darby I arrived in Shropshire, and probably one of the most radically altered communities in the entire New Town. Stirchley, Randlay and Hinkshay, places of which there seem to be comparatively few historic photographs, are covered next, followed by Dawley (including Little Dawley), Horsehay and Lightmoor. In the Ironbridge Gorge itself, selection has been a question of what to leave out rather than what to put in. Not only did the outstanding natural scenery attract photographers such as Francis Frith, who produced a disproportionate number of views compared to many larger towns, but the Coalbrookdale Company also had its own Photographic Department whose staff seemed to have practised their skills throughout the area. The Iron Bridge, needless to say, has been photographed from every conceivable angle since the camera was invented, whilst the lure of the river has ensured that the communities of Coalport and Jackfield have also been well recorded.

With space for captions limited, it is possible to include only the minimum amount of historical information. Those seeking more are recommended to consult Barrie Trinder's excellent *Industrial Revolution in Shropshire*, the *Victoria County History of Shropshire*, volume XI covering Telford and, for more recent events, *Telford: the making of Shropshire's new town* by Maurice de Soissons.

The compilers trust that these photographs will give as much pleasure to those reading this book as they have done to those who put it together. A companion volume, *North Telford*, covers the area north of the M54 and Telford Town Centre.

John Powell
Coalbrookdale, May 1995

Lum Hole Dingle, at the top of Coalbrookdale, was a popular beauty spot a hundred years ago. This is probably mother and son posing, while father is taking the photograph.

One
Madeley

This crowd had gathered outside the Anstice Hall in Madeley in 1910 to celebrate the accession of King George V. Many children are wearing red, white and blue ribbons on their lapels, and local shops are decorated with patriotic flags.

A fine row of buildings on the corner of High Street and Court Street, Madeley just before the First World War. What would the three working class girls in front of Jones's shop window think of the smartly turned out boy with the wicker basket from a more prosperous family?

Not a vehicle in sight. Court Street, Madeley looking due south to the town centre almost a hundred years ago.

One of the earliest photographs of Madeley, probably taken in the 1870s, showing Bryan's impressive shop front on High Street. The people would have been specially posed for the long camera exposure needed.

Madeley Mill, which was situated just north of the present Blists Hill Museum, was engulfed by floodwater from a burst culvert in the 1930s. The firm of G.H. York of Wellington were called in, and had set up equipment to pump away the water when this picture was taken.

The mill seen from the other side after pumping had been completed. The former position of the waterwheel, just to the left of the cast-iron pipe, can be discerned. A rather fine motor car of the period is parked in the lane alongside.

The front steps of the Anstice Hall are seen in this 1930s photograph of an Armistice Day parade. This elegant building is now submerged in the 1960s Madeley Shopping Centre.

Park Street, Madeley looking south east towards Ironbridge about 80 years ago. The bay windows and the porch on the house nearest the camera would have been added comparatively recently to 'modernise' the facade, the equivalent of today's fad for plastic windows.

Madeley from St Michael's Church tower, captured by the *Shropshire Star and Journal* photographer in May 1967 before the centre was altered by the New Town Corporation. Park Street is still a through road in front of Anstice Hall in the background.

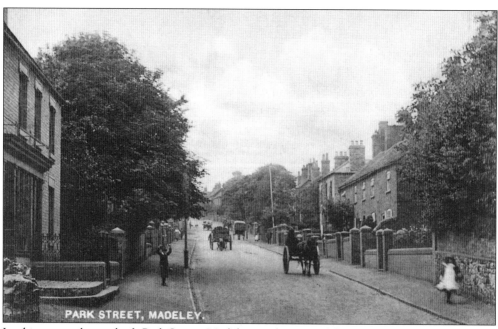

PARK STREET, MADELEY.

Looking west along a leafy Park Street, Madeley, at the turn of the century.

High Street, Madeley, looking west *c*. 1890, with the Royal Oak on the right hand side. Children have gathered to watch the photographer, but ladies window-shopping further up the street are taking no notice.

Timber-framed buildings in Telford are rare, unlike elsewhere in Shropshire, and this example sandwiched between later brick structures in Queen Street, Madeley, was probably 300 years old when this photograph was taken in March 1963.

Gasworks were traditionally located on the outskirts of towns, to protect residents from the smoke and unpleasant smells such places generated. Madeley Gasworks was off Hills Lane and, in this view looking north west early this century, the chimneys of Madeley Court Works can be seen in the distance, to the left of the tree.

W.H. Griffiths of Coalport, who donated the land, is seen laying the foundation stone of the original Madeley Rest Room in Park Avenue on 10 October 1933. R.N. Moore, whose work led to the establishment of the Rest Room, looks on from the right.

Smith's well-stocked outfitting and millinery shop on High Street, Madeley, about eighty years ago. Everything in the window has a price tag, many items labelled – 'special value', or 'cheap'.

No. 64 High Street, Madeley, in the 1920s.

The Hay Farm around the turn of the century. Dating from the eighteenth century, the farmhouse was occupied from about 1775 by Abraham Darby III, who would have been able to watch progress on the building of the Iron Bridge from its windows. The farm is now incorporated into an hotel and country club.

Driver's muddy eye-view of High Street, Madeley, in 1968 looking west from beneath the old railway bridge near the present roundabout with Parkway and Legge's Way.

The Three Horse Shoes, Court Street, Madeley, photographed on 25 September 1968 shortly before demolition.

Total transformation. View looking east from the railway bridge at the bottom of Madeley High Street in 1963 along Bridge Street towards the junction with Queen Street. Now the site of Madeley Roundabout, where the Parkway comes in from the left, Legge's Way from the right and Kemberton Road from the north east.

Madeley cricket team in 1922. If the umpire, rear left, and the scorer, front right, perform only these functions, then the distinguished gentleman in the trilby hat must be a playing member of the eleven.

Six likely lads at Madeley Market railway station on the Coalport branch in 1917. The steam locomotive behind them was one of the London & North Western Railway's most numerous types, this example built in November 1872 and scrapped in March 1927.

Madeley Town Football Club with some of their trophies on display in 1925. The very strong footballing tradition in Ironbridge and Madeley at this time led to the emergence of Billy Wright, the legendary captain of Wolverhampton Wanderers and England during the 1950s.

Track gangers, engine crew, station staff and several others, all looking very serious, have gathered for this photo at Madeley (Salop) Station c. 1890. This station, closed to passengers c. 1925, was near Madeley Court on the Great Western line from Madeley Junction, still in use by coal trains heading for Ironbridge Power Station.

Miss A. Farmer and Miss M. Farmer of Madeley, photographed in September, 1861.

It is difficult to deduce from their fancy dress what play was being performed by this group from the Madeley Church Guild in the 1920s. The man in the top hat has an impressive false beard, and is holding a Broseley clay pipe.

Coalport Road, Madeley better known to locals as Dabbley Lane. The wall on the right separates the Coalport railway line from the road. This flood at the beginning of June 1924 was caused after a night of torrential rain, when widespread damage was caused throughout the area.

Anstice Square, the modern heart of Madeley created in the 1960s. The shops on the left are on the alignment of the old Park Avenue, whilst the library on the right is adjacent to the truncated end of Russell Street.

Tweedale Industrial Estate, looking south in the late 1960s, with Sutton Hill visible top left. The former Wellington to Coalport railway line, later the Silkin Way, can be seen skirting round Madeley, where the Parkway is under construction.

Another view of the new order in the centre of Madeley, showing Russell Square and the ramp leading up to the library, all part of the two-phase redevelopment of the town which occurred in 1969–76.

No, it's not a model, but an aerial photograph of a newly-completed Woodside Estate before any trees had grown to soften the impact of this large-scale development. Looking north, the perimeter road is bottom left. Waverley is on the extreme right, then, moving west, comes Wellsfield, Wigmores, Woodcroft, Wayside and Waltondale.

By the time this photograph was taken after the First World War, the main part of the once impressive Madeley Court, occupied by Abraham Darby I when he was establishing his iron works in Coalbrookdale in the early 1700s, was falling into ruin. The main structure shown here started life in the thirteenth century and then probably had new windows inserted when the porch to the right was built in the sixteenth century.

Packing the annealing oven at Madeley Court Works in the 1930s.

The favourite view of Madeley Court has always been across the pool, but photographs like this one always managed to disguise the decay. By the time Telford Development Corporation began renovation work in the late 1970s, the right hand section of the complex shown here had completely collapsed. Today these buildings along with the gatehouse have been returned to something like their former glory.

Remains of the intricate transport system consisting of canal, plateways and railway which once served the Madeley Court Works, seen here in the 1950s. One of these bridges has now been filled in to carry the Silkin Way, from which the other is still just visible.

Though called into action only rarely, the mines rescue team had to be ready at a moment's notice, just in case disaster should strike. The Madeley Wood Company's Kemberton team show off their breathing apparatus and other equipment in 1913.

Three beam engines for winding and pumping are visible in this view of Madeley Court Colliery c. 1905, and there were several more nearby. The pithead was close to Madeley Court House and extensive spoil heaps, now wooded over, can still be seen near Madeley Court School.

Kemberton Colliery was not located in the village of that name, but was north east of the Cuckoo Oak, Madeley. Miners are pictured on the last day of operation, 26 July 1967. Some of them transferred to Granville, which then became the only deep mine left in the coalfield.

Demolition of Kemberton Colliery headgear on 13 March 1968. Some ancillary buildings survived into the 1980s, but there is now little remaining on the site.

The Madeley Wood Company's blast furnaces in the 1870s, looking north east towards the slopes now occupied by Sutton Hill. Known to some locals as "Blessers Hill" or "Blests Hill", the name Blists Hill had appeared on large scale Ordnance Survey maps by the 1880s, and was adopted as the name of the open air museum which is now on the site.

Removal of a massive egg-ended boiler from Blists Hill by Screen Bros Ltd of Oldbury. The exact date is not known, but is thought to be around the time of the First World War, the furnaces having been blown out in 1912.

30

Two
Stirchley, Randlay and Hinkshay

Beautifully staged photograph of Stirchley Village dating from the last century, with local schoolchildren lined up against the wall beyond the labourers in the foreground. St. James's Church, in the background, was discovered during renovation in 1979 to contain some interesting Medieval wall paintings.

Stirchley School, with a member of staff outside the front porch, about a hundred years ago. "Stirchley School Board Notices" are posted to the left of the door. The building was re-erected at Blists Hill Open Air Museum in 1993.

Pupils of Stirchley School in 1927–8. The names of all the pupils are known, with the exception of the girl second from the right in the fourth row from the front.

Stirchley was still no more than a small village surrounded by open fields when the local hunt met there in the 1950s. The hounds are moving off from the "Rose and Crown" with a few hunt followers in attendance.

Most of the workforce has turned out to pose for this photo of Randlay Brick Works c. 1890. This is a view looking east, with two railway locomotives shunting in the works yard. Randlay Pool, on the right, is now incorporated into Telford Town Park.

In Telford, stone buildings for other than landowners or the more wealthy in society were unusual, but here at Hinkshay is a late eighteenth century row for at least four working class families. Photographed in the 1960s just before demolition.

Hinkshay Rows and New Row, looking south east, with Stirchley Chimney to the left. In the foreground is the Church of England Mission Chapel and, extreme right, the Ever Ready Battery factory. Opened in 1956, this was one of the first new industries to colonise the area though, unfortunately, it closed in the 1990s.

Three
Dawley, Lawley and Newdale

"Captain Webb, the Dawley mon". Born in the town on 19 January 1848, he achieved immortal fame by becoming the first man to swim the English Channel on 24/25 August 1875. He was drowned attempting to swim the rapids at the foot of Niagara Falls on 24 July 1883.

Dawley Church dominates this 1960s view, looking west towards the Wrekin, taken from the top of a pit bank alongside Southall Road. The church dates from 1845, replacing an earlier one which was badly damaged by mining subsidence, despite the building of massive buttresses to try and shore it up.

A Bradford van and a Standard Vanguard car are amongst the obsolete British marques visible in this 1950s view looking north up Dawley High Street towards the "Elephant & Castle".

Though faded and damaged, this photograph portrays a splendid group outside the Market Hall at the north end of Dawley High Street c. 1900. The photographer is facing south. The façade of the Market Hall survives, though somewhat reduced in height.

Before the car became the family's motorised shopping trolley, all your basic requirements from food to clothing, could be purchased within walking distance of your own home. Here is D.A. Pugh's millinery and other fabrics shop in High Street, Dawley probably photographed about eighty years ago.

Postcard dating from the 1920s, showing the Captain Webb memorial at the south end of Dawley High Street. Erected by public subscription, there were over 1,000 in attendance when it was unveiled in 1909. It bears the legend "Nothing great is easy".

Superb S type Sentinel steam lorry operated by Harry Price in the 1930s. Fitted with pneumatic tyres, vehicles like this were capable of 60 m.p.h. This is probably an official photograph by the manufacturer, taken while the lorry was still on test prior to delivery.

Harry Price's fleet of motor lorries, together with drivers, on parade outside the "White Horse" at Heath Hill, Dawley, in the 1930s.

No modern refrigeration at this corrugated iron butcher's shop in Finger Road, Dawley in 1920. This was only part-time employment for the men shown, who also worked in local pits, which is why they are wearing pit boots!

To celebrate the coronation of King George V, towns all over the country marked the event with pageants like this one at Dawley. From the numerous historical scenes re-enacted and posed for the local cameraman, this photograph, with Britannia prominent centre stage, has been selected.

Dawley High Street, looking north, on 26 June 1902, when the entire town was decorated to celebrate the coronation of King Edward VII. A commemorative booklet, containing many photographs including this one, was later produced and sold locally.

Another photograph from the booklet shows the Dawley Town Band leading a procession of nearly 2000 local schoolchildren up the High Street on the same day on their way to the Coronation Grounds, a park which had been specially built as a more permanent reminder of this great occasion.

"Dawley Town" Silver Band
Winners 2nd Prize Madeley
1908

Six years later, the Dawley Town Silver Band were attracting an audience in Madeley, where they were giving a performance in the open air on some kind of wooden stage, presumably erected for the purpose.

41

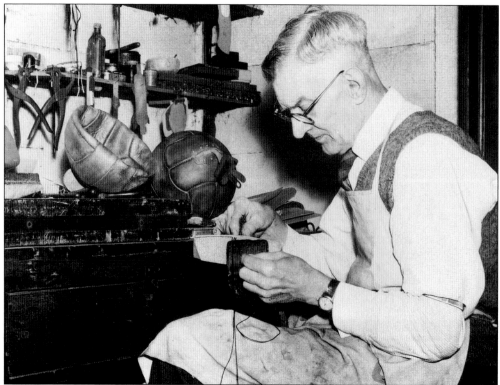

John Thomas Simmonds of Dawley, making a football *c.* 1960, when he was about 70 years of age. The business had been founded by his uncles. J.T. Simmonds was also postman for Lawley Bank.

PC Rowland (PC 160) supervises a cycling proficiency test in Dawley *c.* 1941.

D.A. Pugh, the licensee, stands in the doorway of the "Royal Oak" in George Street, Dawley, early this century.

Mr Pugh poses behind the bar inside the "Royal Oak". This was before the days of optics for serving spirits. Note also the fine handles on the beer machine on the left.

The shop to the left of the Town Hall has been replaced since this view of Dawley was taken some 35 years ago. In the foreground is the Dun Cow Bowling Green, with the pub of that name to the right. The Wrekin is on the horizon.

The country's private railway companies were usually self-sufficient organisations, manufacturing and repairing all their own equipment. But obviously at far away places like Dawley, the London & North Western Railway Company had to rely on Ernest and John Merrington of Finger Road, and their wheelwright Fred Beckett to repair their 4-wheeled dray. A 1911 photograph.

The Dun Cow Bowls Team of 1909, who played on the same green which is in use today (see previous page). Members were from all walks of life, and included a grocer, a draper, a butcher, a rate collector, a schoolmaster, a printer and a postmaster.

Interior of the foundry of J.C. Hulse of Hinkshay Road, Dawley, shortly before closure *c.* 1976. Founded in 1947, the name of the firm will live on in this locality and elsewhere, on the many thousands of drain and manhole covers they manufactured.

Aerial view looking north up Dawley High Street in the 1960s, before pedestrianisation. The modern block which the lorry is passing, currently occupied by Tranter Lowe, is on the site where the buses are parked in the picture shown on page 38.

"'Twas on the Monday morning that the gas man came to call!" He parked his Ford Thames van outside Dawley Library, sometime in the early 1960s.

King Street, Dawley looking towards the junction with New Street and High Street in the 1950s.

Dawley Bank, looking south west towards the Baptist Chapel in the 1950s.

Pool Hill Schools, Dawley, built *c.* 1846 and destroyed by fire in 1977. The distinctive style is similar to that of the warehouse built by the Coalbrookdale Company at Dale End (see pages 90–1) and both are thought to be the work of the same company employee, Samuel Cookson.

The teacher on the right has put on her best hat, and the girls have freshly laundered smocks for this photograph outside Pool Hill School *c.* 1895. Blackboards, with writing still on them, have been put down to keep the benches level.

Squatter cottage dating from *c.* 1830, built on pit waste at Burroughs Bank, Little Dawley. Nine people were living in the cottage in the 1860s. Photographed shortly before its removal to Blists Hill Open Air Museum in the 1970s.

This 1950s photograph seems to capture the rural yet tightly-knit community feel of Dawley before the expansion of the New Town. Looking east along Church Road West with Malinslee church in the background.

Holywell Lane, Little Dawley, looking west towards The Stocking *c.* 1905. This was a squatter settlement, the rather ramshackle cottages springing up from the 1770s onwards on land owned by the Earl of Craven.

Dawley Parva Crossing, on the road between Lightmoor and Little Dawley, seen here in the early 1960s, shortly before the closure to passengers of the Wellington–Much Wenlock line.

An early 1970s view of Holywell Lane, looking downhill to Gravel Leasowes, in the opposite direction to the photograph on the previous page. Some of the cottages were tiny, with bedrooms above ground floor rooms of adjacent dwellings. When the houses were demolished later in the 1970s, there were some families whose forebears had lived in the lane for well over 100 years.

Running water was the exception rather than the rule in the more remote settlements. Here local people are seen collecting water from the Bath Spring, Doseley, early this century, a practice which continued well within living memory. The stand is for placing the full bucket of water on, before transferring it to the top of one's head.

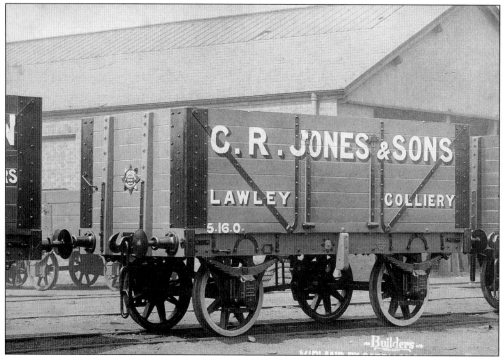

A private-owner wagon belonging to C.R. Jones of Lawley, as seen in the manufacturer's official photograph of *c.* 1910. The Jones family had extensive mining interests in the locality, this C.R. Jones being the same one who operated a brick and tile works at Ladywood, between Ironbridge and Jackfield.

None of the men here from Lawley Social Centre seem particularly pleased to be planting trees in 1934. Was this perhaps a job creation scheme?

The wedding of James Davies and Elizabeth Dabbs, both from Newdale, at St. John's Church, Lawley in 1904. The groom was a wire drawer at the Trench Ironworks.

Pupils have obviously been instructed to pick up their pens for this class photograph at Lawley School on 29 October 1913. The teacher stands at the back on the left, while work continues as normal in the classroom next door.

A turn of the century photograph showing the cottage at Newdale, long since demolished, which was the home of Alice Candlin.

Alice Candlin (later Alice Rickers) left, with her brother William's wedding party outside the same cottage before the First World War. The rings used to train the ivy on the cottage wall are kiln furniture from a local pottery.

Four
Horsehay and Lightmoor

An extremely unusual narrow-gauge plateway locomotive used on the internal railway system at the Horsehay Works. The photograph dates from the 1870s or even earlier.

Horsehay & Dawley Station, looking south in the direction of Lightmoor Junction in the early 1960s. Passenger traffic ceased on this line on 23 July 1962, though freight continued to the Horsehay Works into the 1970s. The platform, minus buildings, is now used by the Telford Horsehay Steam Trust.

Staff at Horsehay & Dawley Station *c.* 1921 include Jack Davies (left), Cis Jones (second left) and Griff Lewis (right), all of whom were signal porters.

The Trustees of Horsehay Wesleyan Chapel in 1936. Back row, left to right, Ernest Biddulph, Flossie Churm, Charles Davies and Bert Lane. Front row, William Ball (left) and Jack Shepherd.

The Horsehay Works were sold off by the Coalbrookdale Company in the 1880s, and later, under the Simpsons, became a successful manufacturer of bridges and other similar engineering structures. This bridge was destined for the Great Indian Peninsula Railway in 1894.

Footbridge for the San Paulo Railway in Florida. Everything made by the company was erected in the works yard and photographed before being dismantled again and despatched to the customer. Houses alongside Horsehay Pool can be seen in the background.

A substantial steel girder bridge for the Central Argentine Railway. Behind it is part of the Cinder Hill, slag left over from a hundred years of ironmaking at Horsehay, which was eventually removed by the Great Western Railway and used for the construction of embankments.

A steam-powered crane in the works yard at Horsehay a hundred years ago. The railway wagon on the left bears the name of Boulton & Co., who had a share in the ownership of Randlay Brick Works with George Wilkinson (see page 33).

Remarkably, the plateway system at Horsehay, which had its origins in the eighteenth century, remained in everyday use until the Second World War. This International tractor, and the horse, shared shunting duties in the 1930s.

Interior view of the Horsehay Works in more recent times. Eventually, the firm became part of Adamson-Butterley, then AB Cranes, and was closed in the 1980s when they concentrated their activities at Ripley in Derbyshire. Much of the site is now cleared and is being used for housing.

The Horsehay Company's works in the 1950s, looking north east. The yard seen on pages 58–59 had been built over by this time. Bridge Road is seen left, before turning into Station Road beyond the Pool. Woodhouse Lane, leading to Doseley, is in the bottom right-hand corner.

Doseley Church, as shown on a postcard dating from *c.* 1910. It is best known as the final resting place of William Ball, the "Shropshire Giant", a 40-stone puddler and shingler at the Horsehay Ironworks who was buried here in 1852. The building was sold and converted into a private house in the 1970s.

Brickworks just south of Station Road, Horsehay, looking north east with Brandlee Chapel to the right. The photograph was taken between 1900 and 1915, during which time the firm operating the works went under the amazing title of Day's Automatic Waste Water Closet & Sanitary Pipe Syndicate Co. Ltd.

West of the previous picture, Station Road, Horsehay is seen running left to right in the centre of this picture of c. 1910, with Pool Hill in the foreground and Heath Hill on the skyline to the left. Most of the properties close to the camera, including the Round House, have long since disappeared.

Close-up of the Round House and attached cottages in the 1930s. This curious residence was a converted kiln, once used to make clay pots for wrought-iron making at Horsehay. It survived well after the Second World War, but unfortunately not quite into the preservation era.

Though damaged, this early twentieth century photograph is of great historic interest. It is the only known view of the trans-shipment shed at Lightmoor where goods were transferred from the horse-drawn plateway wagons, in which the men on the right are sitting, to the standard-gauge railway wagons seen behind them.

Lightmoor Brickworks, looking south in the early 1960s, with the railway from Lightmoor Junction to Coalbrookdale passing from left to right in the middle distance. The top of the hill in the distance is now covered by the Woodside Estate and more recent housing in the Rough Park area. Despite new investment in the 1980s, the brickworks closed in 1991, the last in the district.

Looking in the opposite direction from the previous photograph fifty years or more earlier, with at least nine chimneys visible at the brickworks. Lightmoor Platform was a wooden construction with corrugated iron "pagoda" huts for waiting rooms.

Primitive Newcomen-type beam engine at a mine in the Lightmoor area, possibly as early as 1860. The beam is made of wood, not metal, and the winding drum with chain is on the right. The man in charge, usually known as the charter master, poses in front of the chimney to the left.

Removing the flywheel from Lightmoor Brickworks in 1929, following the sale of a beam engine located there to Henry Ford for his museum in Dearborn, USA. Repatriated by the Ironbridge Gorge Museum in the 1980s, this Coalbrookdale-built engine must surely be the only one ever to have crossed the Atlantic in both directions!

Five
Coalbrookdale

Though never as prestigious as the one down the road at nearby Jackfield (see page 121), Coalbrookdale boasted its own band in 1909.

One of the earliest photographs of Coalbrookdale, taken at the end of the 1850s. Within a few years a viaduct taking the railway through the Dale from Lightmoor to Buildwas would be built across the Upper Furnace Pool seen here from right to left. The prominent three-storey house – Dale House – was built by Abraham Darby I in 1717.

Cottage at the south end of Teakettle Row, Coalbrookdale in the 1880s, when it was occupied by eleven members of the Marriott family. The entire family emigrated to Australia some years later, with the exception of Frederick Marriott, who remained in the district to become a painter at Maw & Co. in Jackfield.

The Villa, Paradise, Coalbrookdale, provides something of a contrast to the tiny dwelling shown in the previous photograph. Members of the well-known Fox-Davies family are seen sunning themselves in a well-tended garden in the 1860s or 1870s.

It is surprising how durable wood can be. When this timber framed building was erected in the middle of the seventeenth century, Coalbrookdale had not yet gained a national reputation for its iron products, and by the time this photograph was taken at the end of the last century, that reputation was already passing into history.

Another early view of Coalbrookdale before the building of the railway in the 1860s. Holy Trinity Church on the right is obviously still very new, having been consecrated in 1854. In the valley, the huddle of small buildings form part of the Coalbrookdale Company Ironworks.

Holy Trinity Church choir one hundred years ago. From the back to the front row, left to right – Ernest Cowper, Cedric Corfield, Will Fletcher, unknown, James Owen, Richard Jones, unknown, Will Morgan, Frank Johnson, Michael Fletcher, Arthur Fletcher, Arthur Anslow, unknown, Walter Welch, unknown, Robert Boycott, Edward Johnson, Tom Bilk, Revd C.B. Crowe, unknown, James York and Wallace Wall the organist.

The Methodist Chapel in Coalbrookdale, erected in 1785 and named in memory of John Fletcher of Madeley. It survived for a hundred years until replaced by the two-storey red brick chapel which is still on the same spot. The clock tower added to the Coalbrookdale Works in 1843 is visible in the left background.

At one time, an industrial service was a regular event in the calendar at Coalbrookdale Church. Rayburn cookers, Merrythought toys and wire riddles are amongst the items taken into the church for blessing in this 1930s picture.

It is possible to date this view looking south down Coalbrookdale to 1858–9, since the Literary and Scientific Institution (now the Youth Hostel) is under construction on the left. The Lower Furnace Pool on the right has long since been filled in and built over, and the cluster of buildings just beyond it mostly demolished.

Coalbrook from Station

Looking north east from the road to Coalbrookdale railway station probably just before the First World War, with the Coalbrookdale Literary and Scientific Institution prominent in the middle and what was originally built as a maltings and later turned into houses on the right.

Trinity Hall Fire Brigade with their fire engine during the Second World War. Slight damage has obscured one of the faces in the front row.

A newly-built Trinity Hall stands in isolation in this view looking north up Coalbrookdale about 90 years ago. Coalbrookdale Station is visible above the hall, with a maltings in nearby Station Road and another in Dale Road in the foreground.

Coalbrookdale Secondary School seen from the back, probably soon after it opened in 1911. The photographer is standing in Station Road, looking east. Most of the rooftops visible in the distance are cottages on Pan Shop Bank, since demolished.

Wedding group in the garden of a house in Darby Road, Coalbrookdale c. 1923–4. The bride and groom are Mr & Mrs Oswald Pitchford.

Coalbrookdale Boys' School in 1928, with the old cornmill in the background. The teacher on the left is Mr Watkiss from Ironbridge, and the one on the right is Miss Saunders. Some pupils walked in daily from as far afield as Little Dawley and Lightmoor.

Dancing round the maypole inside Coalbrookdale School in 1927. Ken Fowler is the boy nearest the camera on the right hand side, and Bessie Cooper the girl nearest the camera on the left. The names of the others are not recorded.

Was Coalbrookdale ever this well manicured? A spotless Great Western Railway saddle tank locomotive, hauling spotless cream and chocolate coloured carriages, pauses at a spotless Coalbrookdale station at the end of the nineteenth century. To the left are some immaculately kept gardens, and even the trees seemed to be especially well groomed.

The historic heart of the Coalbrookdale Company works seen from the air in the 1930s with some of the workers houses close by. A view looking east from the Cinder Hill and Sunniside.

This ceremony is thought to be the dedication of Coalbrookdale War Memorial on 22 May 1921. The memorial, made of bronze, was manufactured at the nearby Coalbrookdale Works. The inscription "Literary and Scientific Institution" on the building was removed when the roof was altered some years later.

Procession passing The Forge, Coalbrookdale, possibly the official party on its way to the ceremony shown in the previous photograph. The houses visible have all since been demolished for road widening.

The Lower Works of the Coalbrookdale Company occupy most of this picture looking north west from the top of Lincoln Hill towards the Wrekin. The photograph was probably taken on a Sunday, since there is little sign of activity and no smoke from any of the chimneys.

The Coalbrookdale Company was the first to use iron railway track and one of the first to build wagons with cast-iron wheels in the middle of the eighteenth century. By the time this photograph was taken almost two hundred years later, the equipment was considered very old fashioned, and looked it, too.

The large number of employees who once worked at The Coalbrookdale Company can be appreciated from this photograph *c.* 1910 showing some of them waiting for their pay packets outside the gates of the Office yard at the Upper Works. The building on the right is the warehouse with the clock tower, now part of the Museum complex.

Coalbrookdale produced munitions during the First World War and aircraft parts during the Second. These four ladies in the Bomb Shop during 1914–18 include Doris Sykes (née Jones) bottom right and Winnie Hall next to her, front left.

The sheer scale of production at the Coalbrookdale Works in times past is exemplified by this photograph, taken off a nineteenth-century glass-plate negative from the firm's own Photographic Department. A conservative estimate suggests that there are over 200 garden rollers here awaiting despatch.

The men involved had the foresight to record this scene for posterity. It was the last day on which a horse was used for shunting goods wagons at the Coalbrookdale Works, the date 21 March 1957 having been chalked on a truck specially for the photograph.

The man in the background has swept the floor spotlessly clean prior to the taking of this very obviously posed picture in front of a steamhammer inside the Coalbrookdale Works . It dates from the 1870s or earlier, and the forging is slung from a crane which can be seen to the right.

The Coalbrookdale Company advertised its wares by means of catalogues and by attending trade shows and exhibitions in the late nineteenth century. Decorative castings, including the statue of the "Eagle Slayer", are seen on their display stand at London Olympia in the 1880s.

Coalbrookdale Works Manager Fred Williams and Lady Bridgeman, beyond the gate on the right, perform the opening ceremony at Allied Ironfounders' Coalbrookdale Museum on 15 October 1959. The invited audience of onlookers are mainly industrialists from the West Midlands iron and steel industry.

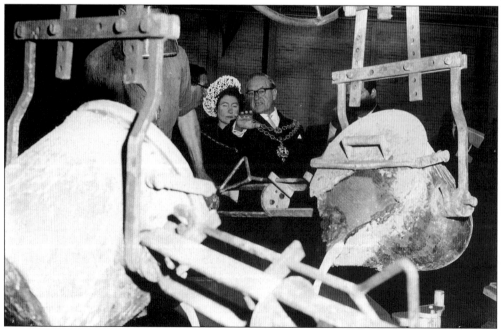

The Lord Mayor of Birmingham during a tour of the Coalbrookdale Works on 30 July 1968.

Six
Ironbridge

The photographer obviously forgot to say "smile please" during one of the regular garden fetes held on the first Wednesday after the August Bank Holiday at Ironbridge Vicarage between the wars. The last fete was held about 1950.

The Albert Edward Bridge carries the railway line from Coalbrookdale across to the south side of the River Severn. Since it was completed in 1863, this view looking towards Ironbridge when it was under construction must date from *c.* 1862. The bridge still carries coal trains to Ironbridge Power Station.

"IRON BRIDGE ANGLING SOCIETY" 1934

Equipment's packed; bus is ready; hopes are high; time for the official group photograph.

Superb reflections from a remarkably calm River Severn enhance this picture of the cable ferry which formerly operated close to the "Meadow" at Ironbridge. It was taken well over 100 years ago, possibly by one of the Maw family, who lived nearby and were keen amateur photographers.

The Severn was completely frozen over when Charles Bagley took his motorcycle and sidecar for a run on the ice near the Albert Edward Bridge on 5 February 1917. William Brown is riding pillion, and his sister is in the sidecar.

Ironbridge "A" Power Station, seen here nearing completion in 1931, was one of the first to supply the National Grid, rather than purely local demand. The site was chosen because of the need for water for cooling, and its construction and operation brought badly needed jobs to the area during the Depression.

The buildings at the south end of Coalbrookdale are dwarfed by this view of the 1960s Ironbridge "B" Power Station, looking south west about 25 years ago. The cooling towers, and the even taller chimney, and the smoke and steam they disgorge, are visible from many miles around.

Looking west towards Buildwas from Dale End, Ironbridge in the 1950s. The rooftops in the foreground are those of now demolished cottages on Pan Shop Bank, whilst the terrace to the south of the main road is now the site of a car park. Chimneys of Ironbridge "A" are visible, though "B" has yet to be built.

Lincoln Hill eaten away by years of limestone working, dominates the west end of Ironbridge in this turn of the century photograph taken from the south side of the River Severn. The river is out of sight in this summertime view, but in winter it would rise within inches of Nailers Row in the foreground, and often flood into the downstairs rooms.

A sizeable fleet of boats was available for hire when this picture of Ironbridge Rowing Club was taken last century. The railway bridge is the one spanning the Buildwas Road near the "Meadow", the Albert Edward Bridge being just out of sight to the left.

Floodwater extends some distance up Coalbrookdale on 10 February 1946, and the son of the local shopkeeper has fun wading through it in his wellingtons. The large maltings, since demolished, accommodated the "Plaza", one of the town's two cinemas.

Rare early photograph of the steam tug *Christiana* moored alongside a trow at the Bower Yard, Ironbridge. This vessel, launched in Shrewsbury in 1858, was used to tow barges with materials for building the Severn Valley Railway, completed in 1862.

This ornate trans-shipment warehouse was built for the Coalbrookdale Company at Dale End, Ironbridge in the 1840s. Following the cessation of river traffic some 40 years later, it was used for a variety of purposes including the manufacture of mineral water at the time this early twentieth century photograph was taken.

The personal freedom for the ordinary man and woman brought about by the introduction of the bicycle has been forgotten since the advent of the motor car. E. Brown's Cycle Works at Dale End, photographed before the First World War, shows Mr Brown himself holding a spanner just outside the front door. Contemporary newspapers record numerous accidents to cyclists on the steep hills in the area.

The pioneering days of motoring are beautifully captured in this picture of Bagley's garage, Dale End, Ironbridge in the 1920s. W. Brown is second from the left, with his wife fourth from left. Mrs Bagley is third from left: her husband is probably the photographer.

The warehouse seen on the previous page had become a garage by the early 1960s, a considerable amount of spoil dumped on the wharves now being used for parking. This spoil was removed and the wharves re-exposed when the building was renovated and converted for museum use in the 1970s.

Long warm summer evenings and tennis on the lawn. This view of Severn House, Ironbridge matches the idyllic image of late Victorian and early Edwardian England so beloved of television costume dramas. This photograph was possibly taken by one of the Maw family who lived in the house, now the "Valley Hotel", for a number of years.

The last member of the Darby family to live in Coalbrookdale was Mrs Frances Muriel Cope-Darby of Sunniside, who died in 1935. Some years earlier, she is seen, third from right, participating in a fancy dress charity collection in Ironbridge. The photograph was taken at the Public Weighbridge, now a garage forecourt, at Dale End. The man on the left is Mr Gem, Mrs Cope-Darby's butler.

A hundred years before the Meadow Inn, Buildwas Road, Ironbridge was transformed into a Swiss Chalet in the 1980s, this is what the building looked like. The proprietor has his own dray for transporting barrels of beer.

High Street, Ironbridge, probably September 1911 if the bill board's proclamation has been correctly interpreted. All the buildings from the clothiers to the one boasting the large gas lamp have gone, replaced by a 'mini roundabout'.

Looking upstream from the Iron Bridge 120 years ago. A trow is moored alongside the south bank, collecting bricks from the brickworks visible on the left. The lime workings on Lincoln Hill can be seen top right, and there are no trees along The Wharfage. These were planted to celebrate the Diamond Jubilee in 1897.

Several vehicles were hit when a runaway lorry heading for Ironbridge Power Station crashed into the river in Ironbridge on 9 April 1947. The driver struggled free, and there were no other casualties. A similar incident, with more disastrous consequences, was to occur at the same spot in 1982, the lorry killing several people when it ploughed into buildings as opposed to the river.

Large waterwheel at a cornmill adjacent to the Benthall Road just south of the Iron Bridge. Often referred to as the Great Wheel of Benthall, it was popular with artists throughout the 19th century, and was photographed by Francis Frith around the turn of the century. The cart in the foreground belongs to Oakley's of Broseley. The wheel, by then disused, went for scrap in the 1930s, though the ruins of the mill survive.

Harry Rogers paddles his coracle past the Co-op on the Wharfage, Ironbridge, during the flood of 10 February 1946. These buildings now house the Tourist Information Centre.

This must be one of the oldest surviving shop fronts in Ironbridge, unaltered in this Victorian photograph when it was probably already sixty years old, it still looks the same today as the Ironbridge Gorge Museum Trust's 'Shop in the Square'.

Another impressive survival is the Tontine Hotel, built directly opposite the Iron Bridge shortly after it opened to traffic in 1781, and then extended to the right by two bays a few years later. A late nineteenth century view.

Ironbridge Market Square in the early 1920s. The most significant alteration to the centre of Ironbridge occurred just after the Second World War when the large three-storey building immediately to the west of the Iron Bridge and seen here to the left of the motor car was demolished. Latterly it housed Bates & Hunts chemists shop.

Ironbridge once had a thriving market which attracted traders and other folk from a wide catchment area. Crowded stalls and numerous carriers' carts feature on this postcard of the Market Place dating from around 1910.

In 1923 the Ironbridge Territorials won the Prince of Wales Shield when away at camp. On their return, it was paraded triumphantly through the town, and is seen being carried from High Street down Waterloo Street, preceded by the band.

Surely one of the strangest sights ever to have been seen on the Iron Bridge, this elephant crossing towards the Broseley side was advertising a circus due to visit the area in the 1920s.

Suitably serious faces are the order of the day for members of Ironbridge Orchestra and Choir, who have had their rehearsal in the Market Hall interrupted for this photograph c. 1895. Seating for the audience is rather spartan and the gas jets, when lit, would provide only a dim light.

A parade heads east through The Square, Ironbridge during a War Weapons Week in World War II. Amongst those on the podium taking the salute is the comedian, Sir George Robey.

Harry Rogers in his coracle poses for the photographer just downstream of the Iron Bridge sometime during the 1940s. The chimney of the White Brickworks is visible beyond the bridge, whilst through the arch can be seen the steam from a train on the Severn Valley Railway.

The toll-keeper on the Iron Bridge in 1921. The Tollhouse survives, though the cottage beyond it has now gone, as has the railway line with its level crossing gates. The bridge remained in use for road traffic until 1934, and tolls were still taken from pedestrians until 1950.

Drilling in the River Severn just downstream of the Iron Bridge in the 1920s. The buildings in the background are on the north side of the river.

The extensive railway sidings at Ironbridge and Broseley Station can be seen on the right in this view looking downstream *c.* 1905. The Free Bridge has yet to be built, and there were gasworks on both sides of the river between Ironbridge and Jackfield.

"Jo see them off."

Ironbridge and Broseley railway station was on the south side of the River Severn opposite the town of Ironbridge and some miles away from Broseley. Here in 1915, the local community have turned out to see their menfolk off to the battlefields of the First World War.

When the Severn Valley Railway opened in 1862, the signalling was rudimentary, but by the turn of the century fine signalboxes like this one at Ironbridge and Broseley station had been provided by the Great Western Railway at all the stations on the line. Unfortunately for the signalmen at Ironbridge, the signalbox faced away from the town and river, so they had only the road up to Broseley to look at between trains.

This was the scene at Ironbridge and Broseley station just after trains had stopped running along the Severn Valley line between Shrewsbury and Bewdley in September 1963. The station's proximity to the Iron Bridge on the left is clear, and beyond in the background are the buildings around Ironbridge Market Square.

Panoramic view of Ironbridge, taken from Bridge Road, Benthall, looking north in the late nineteenth century. The large stone house on the skyline above the church is The Lodge, parts of which date back to the seventeenth century, whilst on the right horizon are the chimneys of the Woodlands Brickworks.

Beddoes hardware shop at the end of High Street, Ironbridge, was purpose built in the 1870s and continued to sell everything a family needed in the way of lighting, pots and pans, iron bedsteads, tin baths, etc. until well after the Second World War. This photograph, probably taken in the 1890s, shows the shop in its heyday. It closed in the 1980s,

Fancy dress in front of the "Block House" in Waterloo Street, Ironbridge, sometime between 1895 and 1910. Unfortunately the reason for the celebration is not known.

Alfred Dixon's shop in High Street, Ironbridge in the 1890s. Not only was he a draper and haberdasher, he also sold boots and shoes and china and glass. "Thomson's Glove-Fitting Corsets" are advertised on the left-hand window.

R.A. Jones's butcher's shop in High Street, Ironbridge, about ninety years ago. No part of the carcasses was wasted, even the pigs' heads being hung up for sale.

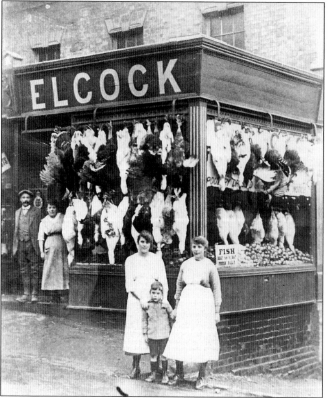

Today the name of Elcock is best known in and around Ironbridge as a firm of coach operators, but early this century the family had a fish and poultry business in Ironbridge. The premises are now occupied by the Central Cafe.

Seven

Coalport and Jackfield

The Coffee House at Coalport in the 1890s. Such establishments were part of the Temperance Movement's efforts to keep working men away from the evils of drink. This one included a newspaper reading room and a small library. It closed *c.* 1917.

New Buildings at The Lloyds consisted of an L-shaped terrace of 16 cottages with outside privies, which are visible in the picture on page 125. This is a view looking from the Coalport end towards Ironbridge. Considered very sub-standard by the early 1960s, when this photograph was taken, they were demolished soon afterwards.

When this photograph was taken from the south bank of the River Severn looking north west at the turn of the century, the Coalport China Works was still a thriving factory employing the majority of the local population. As is apparent in this scene, much of the river bank around the works was made up of millions of broken pieces of china.

Coalport ferry at the foot of the Hay Inclined Plane, which is just visible rising out of sight on the right-hand side, photographed a few years before the Memorial Footbridge was built to replace it in 1922. In the foreground are wasters from the Maw's decorative tile works behind the cameraman in Jackfield.

Jug Row, Coalport, was part of the new town established from the 1790s by William Reynolds around the nearby china works. This view taken c. 1910 is looking north west. The row was demolished in the 1960s, though the "Shakespeare" and other buildings beyond the logs on the left survive.

Decorations in place across Coalport High Street on 24 July 1900 for the visit of the Duchess of York, who later became Queen Mary when George V was on the throne.

China painters at Coalport early this century. One of the men shown emigrated to Canada to seek work when the factory closed, and he took this photograph with him. When he died, his son thoughtfully sent it back to its country of origin.

A mixed group of Coalport workers pictured before the First World War. Though most of the celebrated artists were men, a high proportion of the workforce consisted of women, drawn from Madeley, Jackfield and Broseley as well as Coalport itself.

John Randall, one of the best known of the Coalport artists, who specialised in painting birds. During a life spanning over 100 years, he also achieved recognition as a geologist, local historian and author. On the table beside him can be seen the volume on industry which he contributed to the *Victoria County History of Shropshire*.

John Randall F.G.S. Born Sept 1st 1810. Freedom of the "Borough of Wenlock" conferred June 4th 1909

The fine cast iron bridge at Coalport, which has always had to live in the shadow of its more illustrious neighbour upstream. This pre-First World War view from the "Wood Bridge", looking north west, also shows the railway sheds and sidings north of the tollhouse, and the chapel which has long since disappeared.

A cheerful band of motorcyclists pay their tolls before crossing Coalport Bridge towards Broseley in the 1920s. It appears that wearing your cap backwards on your head isn't a modern fashion after all!

A Severn trow moored opposite Coalport China Works over a hundred years ago, regular river traffic having ceased in the 1880s. This picture was sold locally as a postcard declaring it to be the "last Shropshire trading barge". Recent research suggests that, for some reason, a board has been put above the vessel's name and port of registry to hide the wording "Severn & Canal Carrying Company".

Impromptu photograph taken in 1926 to mark the closure of Coalport China Works. The tall gentleman with the apron, to the right of the lorry, is thought to be its owner, Stephen Triner. Fifty years later, in 1976, parts of the old works were opened to the public as a museum.

An Austin Somerset, a Vauxhall Velox and a Ford Popular give a distinct 1950s feel to this view of the "Brewery Inn" at Coalport. The coach on the right could well have brought fishermen, for whom this stretch of the river is still a favourite destination.

After closure of the China Works in 1926, the site was given over to other industrial purposes, including the manufacture of rubber matting by Nuway. Here a major consignment is seen on its way from Coalport in 1951, destined for the "Campania" on Woodhall's lorries.

"Good Old Dark Lane" and other chalk graffiti adorns locomotive 40058 hauling trains on the last day of passenger service on the Coalport to Wellington line on 2 June 1952. The branch line train was affectionately known to most locals as "The Dodger".

Close-up of the Coalport ferry boat seen on page 109. It is undergoing repair, as the deck planking is missing and the men are holding woodworking tools. Many Coalport workers used it for getting to and from work, and it was at this spot that the dreadful calamity of 1799 occurred, 28 people being drowned when the ferry overturned at night.

Opening the Coalport–Jackfield footbridge across the River Severn in 1922, in memory of those who died in the First World War. The bridge replaced the ferry which can be seen in the previous photograph.

HRH Princess Margaret visited the area on 28 June 1970. She is seen behind the "Brewery Inn" at Coalport accepting a model of a coracle from Eustace Rogers of Ironbridge, who has also brought along the real thing, made by him in his shed near the Iron Bridge. Sir Frank Price, Chairman of Telford Development Corporation, stands between them.

Jackfield Ferry, later replaced by the Free Bridge in 1909. This view looking downstream shows the chimneys of Jackfield on the right, above the half-timbered "Dog and Duck" public house.

THE OPENING OF THE FREE BRIDGE JACKFIELD JUNE 26 1909

Opening of the Free Bridge 26 June 1909, when it poured with rain. View looking north, with the Jackfield Band leading the procession across to the Madeley Wood side. Officially named the Haynes Memorial Bridge, it acquired its popular name because it was the first way of getting across the river in the Gorge without having to pay a toll.

Wooden formwork in position during the construction of the Free Bridge in 1908–9. The smoke which belched forth from the numerous chimneys of the Jackfield brick and tile works is very apparent in this view.

A Midland Red bus heading for Broseley crosses a Free Bridge being pounded by floodwater in the middle of March, 1947. By this time, there was only a handful of chimneys left in Jackfield.

This Francis Frith photograph from the last century looking north eastwards across Jackfield was widely sold as a postcard, sometimes erroneously entitled "Jackville". The chimneys nearest the camera are those of C.R. Jones's Ladywood brick and tile works, with Hollygrove brick and tile works beyond.

The "Black Swan", Jackfield, looking west about 35 years ago. The Free Bridge is in the background. The cottages beyond the pub have since been demolished and replaced by a row of modern houses.

The land around Jackfield has always been prone to landslips, but flooded mine workings to the south in Broseley worsened the problem and this was the result of the worst subsidence for many years in 1952.

Jackfield has always been famous for its silver band, which is still in existence today. Here, they are seen outside Maw & Co.'s factory in 1926. At this time, the band contained no fewer than five brothers from one family – Cecil, Will, Norman, Edward and Harry Hudson.

St. Mary's Church, Jackfield, better known as the Red Church, was built in 1759, but had fallen into disuse by the late nineteenth century due to subsidence caused by the mining of clay from underneath. John Randall describes the miners as working away "like mice eating into a choice cheese". The picture shows the church in a ruinous state, shortly before its final demolition in August 1960.

Funeral procession of the Revd Robert Scipio de Ricci, Rector of Jackfield from 1910 to 1912, winding its way westwards through the village. Beyond the wall on the left, stacks of bricks and tiles made at the local works wait to be loaded onto the railway.

God and Mammon. On Sundays, Jackfield church fed the souls of local people, whilst during the rest of the week, G.H. Gough provided for the bodies of the residents.

Ferry Road, Jackfield about eighty years ago. The houses here would have been only forty years old when this photograph was taken, and of a considerably higher standard than the majority of domestic buildings in the village.

At the end of Ferry Road, Jackfield is the "Boat Inn", seen here on 4 January 1925 during a particularly severe River Severn winter flood.

Jackfield Home Guard on parade outside the "Boat Inn" in 1941. In the background can be seen Coalport China Works, part of which was occupied by the London firm of Chilcotts Ltd. for the first time in the same year as part of the War effort.

Jackfield Crossing looking north east, shortly after the lifting of the track, which had closed to traffic in 1963. The outside privies of New Buildings at The Lloyds can be seen on the opposite side of the river.

Maw & Co.'s Jackfield Tile Works when still in operation in the late 1950s or early 1960s. Viewed from the north bank of the river, looking south, the house known as The Tuckies, once the home of ironmaster William Reynolds, is plainly visible above the two long ranges of buildings enclosing the works yard.

Mr Cross with his daughter on his right arm, E. Thomas on his left and E. Welsh to her left, photographed in the yard at Craven Dunnill's decorative tile works, Jackfield in 1938. The firm stopped making tiles after the Second World War, and vacated the premises shortly afterwards. The site now houses the Jackfield Tile Museum, part of the Ironbridge Gorge Museum Trust.

Some of the 70-strong workforce, and the factory's pet dog, pose for the camera in January 1970 to mark the closure of Maw & Co.'s tile works at Jackfield. The firm had been the major employer in the village since 1883.

Inside the Mosaic Room at Craven Dunnill's Jackfield tile works about a hundred years ago. The people doing the work are women, but the supervisors looking on are both men!

About half a mile to the east of Maw & Co. was a little settlement known as the Werps. The hamlet of barely a dozen houses has now disappeared without a trace, apart from faded photographs like this one, taken a century ago. Here Henry Potts and his wife pose with their four sons outside the "General Gordon" which Henry ran at this time.

Acknowledgements

The compilers would like to record special thanks to Terry Blud, Denis Fry, Ken Jones and Barrie Trinder for help with this volume, and to David Houlston and Marlene Taylor of D.J. Houlston Photography for providing such an excellent service to the Museum over many years. The Social History Group of the Friends of the Ironbridge Gorge Museum deserves special mention, currently active members not already named being Fred Brian, Jim Cooper, Ruth Crofts, Sheila and Harold Grice, Terry Howells, and Cath and Jack Marshall. Thanks must also go to all participants, both living and deceased, in the Friends Oral History Programme, and their relatives, who have proved such a marvellous source of unique photographs. Whilst it is not possible to credit every single picture (indeed, some donors have requested anonymity) thanks go to Mrs Allan, Brian and Trevor Bagley, Maureen Bond, Ivor Brown, C.E.G. Budd, Mr Bullock, Graham Daniels, Betty Duddell, Margaret Duvaston, Ken and Margaret Fowler, Mr and Mrs Garbett, Michael Hale, Mrs Jones, Dorinda Jones, T. Langford, Mrs Lawrence, Geoffrey Lewis, Miss M.E. McCrea, John Marcham, Ron Miles, Cyril Nicholls, F. Ogden, Mary Onions, Angela Pearson, Les Pugh, Eustace Rogers, Nigel Rowe, Shropshire Star Newspapers, Janet Slack, George Teece, Emyr Thomas, Neville Upton, Wendy Waterson, Mrs K. Watling and Geoff Wheeldon. Colleagues at the Ironbridge Gorge Museum to be thanked for their help and forebearance include Marilyn Higson, Dianna Stiff and volunteer Joyce Hiscox. Joanne Smith has been invaluable, not only for years of conscientiously cataloguing the Museum's pictorial collection, but also for typing and checking captions for this book. Glen Lawes and Peter Jennings are also thanked for backing the project enthusiastically from the outset.